Politics Today

The Labour Party

Stewart Ross

Wayland

F

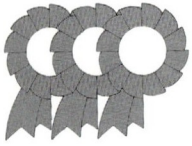

Politics Today

First published in 1986 by
Wayland (Publishers) Ltd
61 Western Road, Hove
East Sussex BN3 1JD

British Library Cataloguing in Publication Data
Ross, Stewart
   The Labour Party. – (Politics today)
   1. Labour Party (Great Britain)
   I. Title   II. Series
   324.24107   JN1129.L32

   ISBN 0–85078–846–3

Phototypeset by
Kalligraphics Ltd, Redhill, Surrey
Printed in Italy by
G. Canale & C.S.p.A., Turin
Bound in the U.K. by
The Bath Press, Avon

Front cover: Neil Kinnock addresses the Labour Party Conference

21115171J

TS

Contents

The Labour Party

The Labour Party has been one of the major forces in British politics in the twentieth century. Eight times it has formed a government after a general election, and it has produced four Prime Ministers. At the 1983 general election, almost 8,500,000 people voted for its candidates, and the party won 209 of the 635 seats in the House of Commons.

For millions of people up and down the country, the Labour Party is the only political party that matters. In their eyes Labour represents the hopes of the poor and underprivileged; it is the party which promises to let *everyone* share in the wealth of the country. Its appeal is traditionally very strong in Wales, the North of England, and Scotland, the less prosperous areas of Britain.

Neil Kinnock, who as leader of the Labour Party is the focus for the hopes and aspirations of millions of British people.

The Labour Party is a relatively new party; it did not form its first government until 1924, and it was not strong enough to have full control of Parliament until 1945. Yet, in or out of power, Labour has had a tremendous impact on modern Britain. The Welfare State, our system of secondary education and the great nationalized industries all owe their existence to Labour policies.

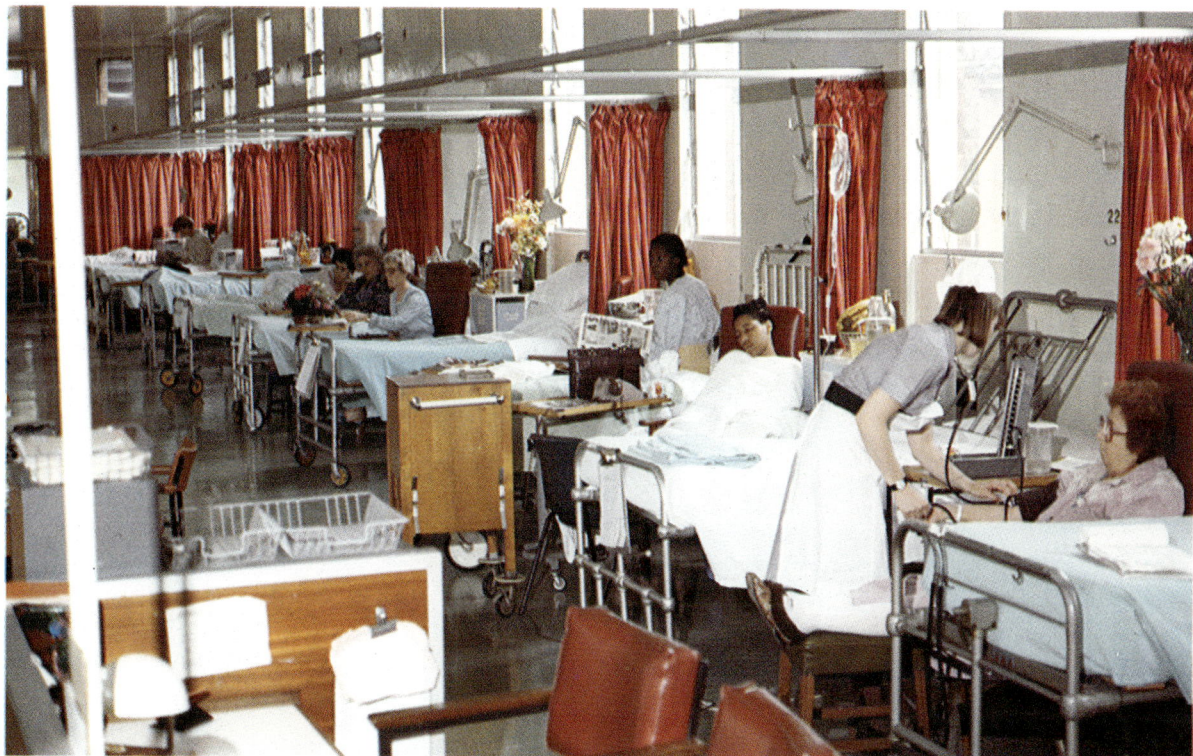

Britain's National Health Service was introduced by Labour in order to provide free 'treatment of every kind to every citizen without exceptions'.

In the late 1970s and the early 1980s, Labour has been in difficulty. Its members have disagreed with each other in public, it has lost two general elections, and some of its members have left to form the Social Democratic Party. Nevertheless, Labour has done as much as any other party to create modern Britain, and will no doubt continue to shape and influence our society in many different ways in the future.

The Rise of Labour

By the end of the nineteenth century, many members of the working classes felt that their wishes were not being truly represented by the two major political parties of the time, the Liberals and the Conservatives. Therefore, in February 1900, the trade unions joined with various socialist groups to form the Labour Representation Committee. Six years later, they won twenty-nine parliamentary seats and changed their name to the Labour Party.

In the years that followed, the party's popularity grew so rapidly that Ramsay MacDonald was able to form the first Labour government in 1924.

Ramsay MacDonald (left), whose efforts did much to make Labour a unified political party. He subsequently damaged party unity by leading a coalition government with Tory and Liberal support.

Although this government was short-lived, MacDonald was back in office in 1929. This second Labour government collapsed over differences as to how to deal with the worldwide slump in trade, and Labour remained out of office until after the Second World War.

In 1945, Labour won an overall majority in a national election for the first time. Prime Minister Attlee introduced a policy of socialist reform, which brought better housing, health care and education for millions of people. Attlee lost power in 1951, but under Harold Wilson in the 1960s and 1970s, it began to look as if Labour was the natural party of government. The election of the Conservatives in 1979, however, brought an end to Labour's run of successes.

Since 1979 the Labour Party has been forced to examine its organization and principles very carefully. It has tried to bring itself up to date by creating a more progressive image, which will appeal to the skilled working class and the middle class, as well as its traditional supporters.

Harold Wilson, who in his career was Prime Minister for a total of eight years, led the party during one of the most successful periods in its history.

Policies

At the heart of Labour policies lies the idea of socialism. To the Labour Party this means a controlled alteration of our society into one in which there are no class distinctions, in which wealth is shared out more evenly and in which businesses and industries are owned by the nation as a whole rather than by individuals. Behind this is a spirit of comradeship and a belief in the equal worth of each individual, regardless of age, race or sex.

The Labour Party looks to central government, rather than individuals, to change society, believing that 'Freedom obtained at someone else's expense is not freedom at all, but tyranny.' (Labour Party 1985 leaflet) Labour sees it as the government's task to protect the weak from the

Coal-miners in South Wales. The Labour Party is pledged to increase State support for Britain's nationalized industries, such as coal and steel.

strong. In practical terms it plans to tax the wealthy heavily so that their money is shared among the poorer sections of the community. It also wants the State to own major industries, including the banks and the public transport system.

A Labour government would increase spending on the health service and education, abolishing private schools. The party believes unemployment to be a more serious problem than inflation, and would introduce policies to create jobs, even at the risk of increasing prices.

Labour would like to see increased spending on State education, with private schools eventually being abolished.

The EEC is not popular with Labour, many of whose supporters would like to see Britain leave a community which, they believe, is primarily an organization to help businessmen. As far as defence policy is concerned, Labour is in favour of reducing expenditure on arms and perhaps of declaring unilateral nuclear disarmament.

Labour in Government

Under different leaders, the Labour Party has pursued different aims, but its general policies have on the whole been consistent. The party has always seen it as its duty to create a fairer, less divided society.

Ramsay MacDonald's governments achieved few lasting socialist goals because they did not have overall majorities in the House of Commons, but they did have an effect foreign policy. During the Second World War, Labour supported Churchill's coalition government and several of its members were brought into the cabinet. Despite the party's reputation for seeking to avoid armed conflict, Labour's resolve to resist Hitler's

The Labour government of 1924. Few of its members were experienced in affairs of state and it was therefore unable to accomplish many of its economic and social objectives.

Germany was unwavering.

It was under Clement Attlee in the years following the war that a Labour government perhaps accomplished more of its aims than at any other time. Large-scale nationalization – of industries, utilities and communications – and the creation of the National Health Service, which was free to all, were rapidly introduced. These policies changed the shape of Britain's society, and permanently altered the expectations of its people.

Since Attlee's government, Labour has introduced the system of comprehensive education and has provided many State benefits to the underprivileged. Through close co-operation with the trade unions, the party has sought to cushion the country against the unemployment and social deprivation that have arisen as traditional industries go into decline. Opponents say Labour policies have been unrealistic, but the party remains committed to its socialist path.

Clement Attlee (centre) after his election as Prime Minister in 1945. His government lasted six years, in which time many sweeping reforms were carried out.

Party Structure

The Labour Party grew, like a plant, from its roots of local societies. These existed long before the party had any MPs, so unlike the Conservative Party, there is a feeling that local groups are the true representatives of the movement.

All party members in a given area belong to their local Labour Party branch. Several branches serve a constituency, which is run by General and Executive Committees. The constituency groups usually have close links with trade unions and other like-minded organizations, such as the Young Socialists. The principal responsibility of constituency parties is to select, at local level, Labour parliamentary candidates.

The party headquarters in London.

Perhaps the most important element in the party's structure is the National Executive Committee. This committee of twenty-eight people, representing all sections of the party (unions, constituencies, MPs, women's groups and socialist societies) is responsible for running the party conference. To carry out the committee's decisions there is a large staff at the party's headquarters (150 Walworth Road, London) under the control of the General Secretary.

The party's headquarters have recently been reorganized to cope with the demands of modern politics. Taking a lead from the Conservatives, the party now takes great care over its publicity. The headquarters have been transformed into an efficient administrative body that is ready to guide the party into the modern world of television studios, credit cards and slick advertising.

The headquarters staff are responsible for the day-to-day administration of the party.

Labour Party Finance

Running a political party is very expensive. Labour receives most of its money from the trade unions. In 1982 the total raised by the party was £3.9 million, of which £2.8 million came from the unions. After seeking the approval of their members through a ballot, trade unions can affiliate themselves to the National Executive Committee for a fee of 50p per member (1983). If they want, they can pay more fees than they have members, as the AUEW (Amalgamated Union of Engineering Workers) did in 1982.

Unions can also pay money to the party at the constituency level, by sponsoring candidates at an

James Callaghan addresses the Trades Union Congress in 1980. Labour has always had a close working relationship with the unions.

A press conference to launch the Labour Party campaign in the 1981 local government elections. Much of the party's money is spent on this sort of publicity.

election. In 1983 this cost an average of £2,927 for each candidate. Other funds come from individual party membership fees, although this source of income has declined in recent years (see page 24). While Labour is in opposition in Parliament, it also receives State aid: £105,000 in 1984.

Although Labour does not have financial resources to match those of the Conservative Party, which receives a great deal of money from private companies, the gap is narrowing. In the 1950s the Tories had over three times as much money as Labour; now the gap is only about 30 per cent.

Where does the money go? The running of the party headquarters costs over £300,000 a year. The rest of the party's £4 million annual income goes on political broadcasts, printed publicity, opinion polls, the conference and a host of other activities expected of a modern political party.

15

Labour and the Unions

For centuries British craftsmen and workers have had their own representative groups, beginning with the medieval guilds, but the Industrial Revolution brought the need for stronger workers' organizations. The trade unions satisfied this need and, as we have seen, the Labour Party

An early trades union membership certificate. The organization of workers into unions was a key factor in the creation and growth of the Labour Party.

Arthur Scargill, President of the National Union of Mineworkers, addresses the Labour Party Conference. The unions expect to receive support from Labour in return for the money they put into the party.

grew out of the unions' wish to have working people directly represented in Parliament. From the beginning, therefore, trade unions have played a major part in the organization and running of the Labour Party.

Trade unions provide the Labour Party with most of its money (see page 14) and therefore they demand a proportional say in party affairs. Union representatives are the largest single group, with twelve delegates, on the party's ruling National Executive Committee. When the party leader is chosen, the unions have the largest vote in the electoral college (see page 18). However, it is at the party conference that union influence is seen at its strongest.

Issues are decided at the Labour Party Conference by vote. The counting of the votes does not depend upon the number of people in the hall, but upon how many Labour Party members are represented by those present. So the delegation from the Transport and General Workers Union (TGWU) can cast about 1.2 million votes, that being the number of Labour Party affiliation fees the union pays. Since the total party membership is about 6.2 million, the power of the TGWU is considerable.

The Leader

The task of leading the Labour Party requires the highest political skills. Perhaps more than the leader of any other major party, the Labour leader is subject to continual pressures from different groups within his party, and keeping these forces balanced and loyal to him can be a very tricky business.

Labour chooses its leader through an electoral college. This college is not a building, but a group of Labour Party members, 40 per cent of whom are trade union representatives, 30 per cent Labour MPs and 30 per cent constituency party representatives. The advantage of this system is that it means the eventual leader has support from a wide cross-section of the movement, and not just from the MPs, for example.

The party leader and his deputy sit on the

A Young Socialist rally in 1964. There are a number of different groups within the Labour Party, each with their own priorities and each attempting to influence the leadership.

National Executive Committee, and play a major part in determining party policy. The leader has the final say over what goes into the Labour manifesto, the official statement of policy produced before each election. When the party is in power, the leader can select his own Cabinet, but in opposition the Parliamentary Labour Party elects a Parliamentary Committee, from which the leader picks his Shadow Cabinet (see page 21).

Despite the pressures they face, Labour leaders have survived longer than their Conservative counterparts. It is possible, however, that the job is becoming still more demanding: the party had four leaders in the decade 1976–1985.

Neil Kinnock and Roy Hattersley after their 1983 election as party leader and deputy leader respectively. Kinnock was the first Labour leader to be chosen under the electoral college system.

Labour at Westminster

However active a party may be in the constituencies or at its conference, in the end its aim must be to win an election and control the House of Commons. When in opposition, Labour's job at Westminster is to criticise the government and put forward its own alternative policies in as attractive a manner as possible. When in power, the party's task is to support the government and see that party policy is put into effect.

The Labour Party has been in opposition since 1979, having twice lost general elections to Margaret Thatcher's Conservatives. Since the 1983 election Labour has had 209 MPs in the Com-

The Houses of Parliament in London. Since 1983 the Labour Party has had 209 MPs, out of a total of 635 in the House of Commons.

mons, while 130 peers also support Labour in the House of Lords.

Labour members of the House of Commons form the Parliamentary Labour Party, which meets once or twice a week (less frequently when Labour is in government) to discuss policy and other matters of interest to its members. MPs also form party committees on issues such as defence and education, and some belong to all-party groups concerned with topics as varied as football and films.

Roy Hattersley, the deputy leader of the party, is also Labour's shadow Chancellor of the Exchequer.

When the party is in opposition, there is still a lot of work to be done by the MPs. A handful of Labour MPs are shadow spokesmen, each of whom has to keep a close watch on a government department and give Labour's view on matters concerning that department. Roy Hattersley, for example, is currently Labour's shadow Chancellor of the Exchequer. The shadow spokesmen are normally chosen from an elected Parliamentary Committee of twelve members.

Who Votes Labour?

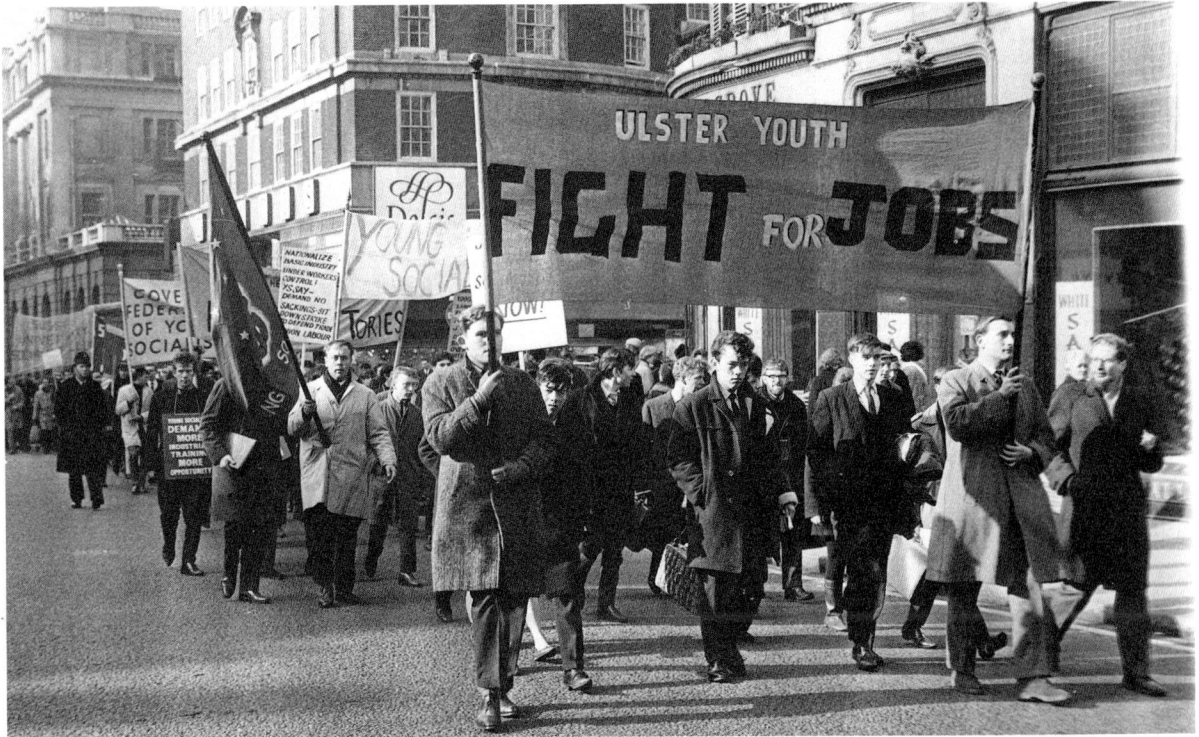

Traditionally Labour has been the party of the working class, and the party's call for the redistribution of wealth and the limitation of privilege has a great appeal to the more deprived sections of our community. But just to call Labour the party of the working class is too simple.

In 1983, around 4 million working-class people voted for the Conservatives, while many wealthier, middle-class voters gave their support to Labour. The reason why it is difficult to say exactly which type of person votes Labour is that British society and politics are changing quite rapidly. Fewer people now consider themselves working class, and in the 1980s the emergence of

Labour has always attracted large-scale support from the young, particularly in areas outside the South East.

the SDP/Liberal Alliance has given voters more choice in elections. We can, however, make some generalizations about the sort of people who tend to vote Labour.

Labour's support is much stronger in the north than in the south; the party holds no seats south of a line drawn from Bristol to London. Its appeal tends to be greater to men than to women, and to the young rather than the old. Labour voters are often members of trade unions who do not own their own homes. Frequently they work for local government or State-owned industries. The party also has a following among students and young professional voters.

Minority groups, such as immigrants, also look to the Labour Party to protect their interests. There was recently a campaign to persuade the Labour Party Conference to accept black people as a special category within the party.

Many members of Britain's black community are Labour voters. Recently there have been moves to encourage more Blacks to participate in the running of the party.

Party Activists

The great majority of British people play almost no part in politics. About 25 per cent do not even bother to vote in elections, and less than 5 per cent belong to a political party. Those who are politically active, therefore, are not representative of the population as a whole, or of their party, to whichever one they belong. Labour Party activists tend to be more middle class and have better educational qualifications than the average Labour voter. They are also more left-wing.

Ken Livingstone has risen to prominence through his career in local politics in London. There is a tradition in the party that local activists are the true representatives of the socialist cause.

The majority of Labour Party members (of whom there are almost 6 million) are affiliated through a trade union. Since the 1950s the number of individual party members has fallen from about 1 million to just over 300,000, although these individuals are very often highly committed to the political cause.

Tony Benn, one of the leading figures on the left wing of the party. Benn probably commands more support from party activists than any other senior Labour politician.

The Labour Party is a broad organization, so its members often have differing views on how the party should conduct itself. Party activists, many of whom belong to groups such as the Young Socialists, often urge the leadership to be more positive, more radical in its socialism. Why, they ask, did the Labour governments of 1964–1970 and 1974–79 not do more to create a socialist society? Their leaders, men like Derek Hatton and Tony Benn, say that Labour has declined in popularity because it has abandoned its socialist principles. Squabbles between party activists and more traditional Labour politicians, such as Neil Kinnock and Roy Hattersley, about the policies of a future Labour government have recently done much to spoil the party's image.

Selection of Candidates

Nowhere are the differences between traditional Labour politicians and the activists more clearly to be seen than in the process of selecting Labour candidates. In 1981 the process was changed in favour of the constituency parties, and several Labour MPs left the party to form the SDP.

Labour candidates are now chosen by the constituency parties. In theory the National Executive Committee has a veto, but this is almost never used. In 1981 the party's leader, Michael Foot, vetoed the selection of the militant Peter Tatchell as the candidate for Bermondsey. Foot later changed his mind, but nevertheless, the incident caused an uproar within the party.

Peter Tatchell (left), canvassing support during the Bermondsey by-election in February 1983. Many people thought the party should be represented by a more 'traditional', and local, candidate.

Candidates have to be put forward for selection by a group attached to the local party, such as a trade union. Trade union candidates usually stand a high chance of being selected because the union is able to sponsor them. The final choice is made by the constituency party's General Management Committee, which tests the prospective candidates' grasp of party policy, ability to speak in public and other practical qualities.

A meeting of the National Executive Committee. Although the committee is one of the most powerful forces in the Labour Party, its veto over the selection of party candidates is seldom used.

Even after they are selected as candidates and elected to Parliament, Labour MPs are still answerable to their local party members whom they represent at Westminster. Before the next election they have to be reselected. Several MPs have found themselves replaced because their behaviour at Westminster did not conform to the wishes of their local party.

Conference

The Labour Conference is the most important event in the party's year. It is held in a major resort, such as Blackpool or Brighton, lasts for five days, and all its important proceedings are televised. The party is on show to the nation, but, unlike the Conservatives', Labour's conference is not so much a publicity exercise as a genuine political meeting. Discussion and disagreement, argument and applause are all on display to the press and the television cameras.

Each organization affiliated to the Labour Party is entitled to send delegates to conference, one delegate being admitted for every 5,000 members. Over 1,000 people, drawn from the trade unions, the Parliamentary Labour Party, the Co-operative Movement and other organizations, usually attend the conference. All voting is done by 'block

The votes cast at the Labour Conference have a major influence on party policy.

28

vote' (see page 17).

The purpose of the conference is to bring the party together and to provide an opportunity for all its branches to meet. It also debates and votes on party policy. Some claim that the conference is 'the final authority of the Labour Party'. Labour governments, on the other hand, while trying to implement conference's wishes, have sometimes refused to be bound by them. In 1975, for example, the Labour government ignored their conference's hostility towards the EEC.

At the end of the conference, with the argument and voting behind them, delegates unite to sing 'the Red Flag'. This emotional ending to the conference reminds delegates and onlookers alike of the warm, crusading spirit which has characterized the Labour Party since its birth.

Representatives from all sections of the Labour Movement gather each year at the conference, to discuss policy and once more to affirm the party's commitment to the socialist cause.

Important Dates

1900   Labour Representation Committee formed.

1906   29 LRC MPs returned at the general election.

1918   63 Labour Party MPs returned at the general election.

1922   142 Labour Party MPs win seats in the Commons.

1924   Ramsay MacDonald forms minority Labour government which lasts for nine months.

1931   Labour's second minority government splits on the issue of cutting unemployment benefit. Labour Prime Minister Ramsay MacDonald forms a national government.

1940   Labour leaders join Churchill's wartime coalition government.

1945   Labour, under Clement Attlee, wins the general election with an overall majority (146) for the first time.

1950   Labour's majority cut to 5 in the general election.

1951   After several Cabinet resignations, Labour loses the general election.

1955   Hugh Gaitskell elected Labour leader after a general election defeat.

1963   Harold Wilson elected Labour leader after the death of Gaitskell.

1964   Labour under Harold Wilson wins the general election with a 4-seat majority.

1966   Harold Wilson increases the Labour majority to 96.

1970   Labour loses the general election to Edward Heath's Conservative Party.

1974   Harold Wilson defeats the Conservatives in two general elections (February and October), winning an overall majority of 6 in the second election.

1976   Harold Wilson resigns and is replaced by James Callaghan as Labour Prime Minister.

1979   Labour loses the general election.

1983   New Labour leader Michael Foot loses the general election. Neil Kinnock is the first Labour leader to be elected through an electoral college.

Further Reading

Ball, A. R., *British Political Parties* (Macmillan, 1981)

Blondel, J., *Voters, Parties and Leaders* (Penguin, 1974)

Butler, D. and Kavanagh, D., *The British Election in 1983* (Macmillan, 1984)

Coxall, W. N., *Parties and Pressure Groups* (Longman, 1981)

Rose, R., *Do Parties Make a Difference?* (Macmillan, 1980)

The New Hope for Britain: Labour's Manifesto, 1983

Warrior, P., *The Political Parties* (Wayland, 1983)

Glossary

Affiliate   Enter into association with.

Cabinet   A group of about twenty-two leading government ministers who advise the Prime Minister.

Chancellor of the Exchequer   The minister responsible for the country's economy.

Coalition   A group made up of people from more than one party.

Constituency   A district represented by an MP.

EEC   The European Economic Community, or Common Market.

Election   The process by which members of the House of Commons, and many other representative bodies, are chosen by voters.

Electorate   All those entitled to vote.

General election   An election for all the seats in the House of Commons.

Left-wing   Strongly socialist.

Manifesto   A declaration of the policies a party intends to carry out.

MPs   Members of Parliament, usually meaning the House of Commons.

Opinion poll   A survey which records people's views on a given subject.

Peer   A member of the House of Lords.

Policy   The path a political group intends to follow.

Prime Minister   The leader of the government.

Radical   Wanting fundamental change.

Seat   A place in the House of Commons.

Slump   A sudden economic collapse.

Sponsor   Support with money.

Tory   Conservative.

Trade union   A group of workers from the same field of employment organized to further their interests in areas such as pay and working conditions.

Veto   The right to stop certain decisions and actions being carried out.

Vote   Make a choice between two or more options.

Welfare State   A society in which the government looks after the basic welfare (health, education, etc.) of all people.

Westminster   The palace in London which houses the Lords and Commons.

Index

Acknowledgements

The publishers would like to thank the following for supplying pictures: Camera Press 20; John Chapman 12, 13; Colorific *cover*; Inner London Education Authority 9; The Labour Party 10, 23; Frank Spooner Pictures 28, 29; Topham 4, 5, 6, 7, 14, 15, 16, 17, 18, 19, 21, 22, 24, 25, 26, 27; TUC Library 11; Wayland Picture Library 8.